SCRIPTURES
for your Thoughts.

By LATANYA N. SMITH

Copyright © 2016 by Latanya N. Smith

Scriptures for your Thoughts.
by Latanya N. Smith

Printed in the United States of America.

ISBN 9781498472579

All rights reserved solely by the author. The author guarantees all contents are original and do not infringe upon the legal rights of any other person or work. No part of this book may be reproduced in any form without the permission of the author. The views expressed in this book are not necessarily those of the publisher.

Unless otherwise indicated, Scripture quotations taken from the King James Version (KJV)—*public domain.*

Scripture quotations taken from the New King James Version (NKJV). Copyright © 1982 by Thomas Nelson, Inc. Used by permission. All rights reserved.

Scripture quotations taken from the Holy Bible, New International Version (NIV). Copyright © 1973, 1978, 1984, 2011 by Biblica, Inc.™. Used by permission. All rights reserved.

www.xulonpress.com

I dedicate this book to my dad,
Richard Morris (*Poppa Smurf*). Why?
Because I'm his "baby girl."

To my family, spiritual family, extended family
and to my new family to come:

Scriptures for your *Thoughts* is a spiritual seed that I pray it gets planted into your souls and spirit and that our Lord and Savior adds His powerful increase. Amen

My Thank Yous

I want to thank my Lord and Savior for giving me this vision and for not dimming this fire that was placed within me years ago. At one point, I thought it was just that *a thought*—a feeling. But I thank God for pressing my heart and my spirit to write this book. I thank Him for giving me the strength to step out of my comfort zone and into a place where I know He wants me to grow and to help others to grow: place of revelation, a place of knowledge, a place of wisdom, and place of faith in Him. I thank you, God, for your love for me. I thank you for calling me your Special One.

I want to thank my mommy, Gladys Smith-Jenkins, for encouraging me to go back to college.

For a brief moment, it only lasted for about a week, I decided not to go back to school because I was out of my comfort zone and I wanted to stay home. Thank you, mommy, for pushing me to go back to college and to get my bachelor's degree from Lincoln University in Oxford, PA. Because of you, I was the first in my family to obtain a college degree; because of this foundation, I stepped out of my comfort zone again and pursued my Master's Degree in Social Administration at Temple University in Philadelphia, PA. Thank you for believing in me. Thank you for your love. Because of the Lord and you, I was able to set the foundation, set the bar, set the guidance for my sisters to pursue their education milestones. I love you dearly.

To my sisters, Pam and Yolanda: Continue to pursue your educational dreams. I believe you will fulfill the purpose that the Lord has for you if you continue to keep Him first. Pam, I believe you will become a licensed nurse; keep believing and keep the faith in God. Yolanda, I really want to call you by your nickname but I won't, I believe you will become a well-educated accountant. Both of you, step out of your comfort zones.

To my one and only brother: Richard, also known as "Stuff," thank you so much for your humor and thank you for sticking to your dreams. You always wanted to work for Septa. When you were younger, you made Septa buses out of Legos; you hung around the bus depots so long and so much that you would bring home pieces of trolley tracks, keys, and other Septa "stuff." Look at you now, a Septa driver and you are loving it.

To my nephew, Domineir: Continue to keep God first and follow the path that He has for you. Your love for trains is setting a path and foundation for your career. I believe in you. You are so dear to my heart. Karen, you are so inspirational and I love you dearly. Thanks for being the best sister-n-law EVER!

To my very dear and close friend, Darlene: I love you girlie. I love your spicy and witty spirit. Your quick "come backs" did rub off on me, and I thank you for that. We have been sisters for years, and I appreciate you so much.

To my spiritual brother Minister Eric "Rick" Greene: You instilled in me to "pay attention to detail." I carry this reminder everywhere I go, and it truly works. It allows me to listen tentatively and to observe closely the things that are happening in my life. You are my big brother, and I thank God for you. Thank you for my first airplane ride to Myrtle Beach and many other travelling experiences. You continue to have my back, and I appreciate your unique love for me. I love you dearly. To "Trina Gal," aka Mrs. Greene, thank you for your transparency and your kindness. You welcomed me into your home and into your life. I love you and thank you.

To my special gems: Ericka Greene, you are my heart and I love you so much. Become the model that you want to be and don't let anyone stop you. You will fulfill your dreams only if you continue to keep God first. Yona, my sweet and beautiful Goddaughter, continue to smile for the Lord and continue to be the best you can be. To Junior, Lici and Aaliyah, thank you for allowing me to be your Aunt Tanya. It is such a joy being part of your lives. Daijah, Deyonnah, Tyler (my Halfpint),

Tyeson—The Smacksonians. I love you so much. I enjoy being your Aunt Tanya and I pray that I have given you Godly examples.

To my Godsons: Pastor Tyrone "TWyse" Smack, Eric "Booty" Greene, and my Irvin Washington. I love you guys so much. You all have pursued your dreams and you are totally blessed by God. Ty, you are my heart and you have helped shape and mold me to be the best woman of God to all those who came my way. You are a true living testimony and I thank God for you. Thank you for allowing me to be part of your life and your family. You took the time to minister to me and to be my friend and for that I am totally grateful. My "Booty Ooty," You are so dear to me. Keep God first in your life and you will be exactly where He wants you to be. Love God, yourself, and your precious gems, Tru and Treasur. It's no accident as to why you named your children these names. Irvin Smirvin, my tall tree Godson, you are such a humble and pleasant man of God. Love cannot explain how I really feel about you. You have a beautiful family, and I wish that you continue to be an example of Christ everywhere you go.

My spiritual family: Quiana Smack, my "QuiBie," Pastor Donald Strickland and his lovely beautiful wife Prophetess Danette Strickland, my spiritual leader Apostle Warren D. Martin, Sr. and his beautiful wife Pastor LaCatherine Martin, my spiritual mother, Sister Rachel, Mr. and Mrs. Bernice and Tyrone Smack, Mr. and Mrs. Carolyn and Major Perry and my Uncle Tim, The Chatmans. You have all contributed various levels of spiritual food into my life. You all have shaped and molded me to be the best I can be in the Lord. I love you all so much. And Quiana, thanks for exposing to me the true meaning of "beautiful."

Brief Introduction

Well, where do I begin? Years ago, the Lord placed it in my spirit to write a book for those who wish to have a scripture handy for their daily thoughts. Thoughts of hate, worry, unfaithfulness, insecurity, love, impatience, those thoughts that we tend to keep within our spirit or mind on a daily basis. I pray that *Scriptures for Your Thoughts* will be a quick reference, a spiritual seed to ease or encourage those who are experiencing life's typical situations, whether they are positive or negative.

Your thoughts

Your thoughts: "But Lord, they are not going to listen to me. They will look at me funny."

Your thoughts: "I pray that I don't go to hell because of my dad's sins."

Your thoughts: "God, I can't. Every time I think something is going my way, something always happens."

Your thoughts: "God, I just want your Will to be manifested in my life. Let your Will be done, Lord. My will is trying to get strong."

Your thoughts: "I'm tired of thinking negatively all the time. I just want peace in my mind."

Your thoughts: "I'm not going to forgive her. I'm good."

Your thoughts: "I'm tired. I just want rest. I'm tired of being worked on by God."

Your thoughts: "I'm fearful."

Your thoughts: "I want revenge! I'm going to get them back."

Your thoughts: "She/he deserves it. Good, that's what he/she gets."

Your thoughts: "I can't believe she got the job. I'm more qualified than she is."

Your thoughts: "I'll trust you, Lord."

Your thoughts: "I need you now, Lord."

Your thoughts: "I want to be an example of my Lord and Savior."

Your thoughts: "My plans never come through." "No matter how much I try, something always comes up." "I knew this would happen." "I can't seem to get ahead."

Your thoughts: "I want to hear from you, Lord."

Your thoughts: "I'm sorry for my sins, Lord. I'm so sorry, Lord. Please forgive me."

Your thoughts: "Lord, please help my friend."

Your thoughts: "I have such a desire to be accepted by others. At times, I even find myself waiting on them to validate or recognize me."

Your thoughts: "Lord, your peace is what I seek. Your strength is what I need right now. Your love is greatly needed to overwhelm this pain".

Your thoughts: "I trust you, Lord"

Your thoughts: "Lord, I know you are comforting me right now, right in the midst of my pain."

Your thoughts: "I have resentment towards them."

Your thoughts: "Dear Lord, I am so confused."

Your thoughts: "No one loves me; no one cares about me."

Your thoughts: "I'm so lonely, Lord. I know you are here with me, but I feel so lonely."

Your thoughts: "He/She gets on my nerves."

Your thoughts: "I'm wondering if they are talking about me."

Your thoughts: "Lord, I want my will to line up with Your will."

Your thoughts: "You make me sick."

Your thoughts: "So you're saying I can't come back to church because I have a tattoo. I'm not coming to this church again."

Your thoughts: "Lord, thank you for your encouraging Word."

Your thoughts: "This is why I don't like praying with you."

Your thoughts: "These people make me sick. They are so rude and unprofessional."

Your thoughts: "Lord, help me to manage my emotions better." "I'm so worried right now." "I'm scared to do it."

Your thoughts: "These people make me sick." "I'm tired of turning the other cheek."

Your thoughts: "Lord, I'm just too scared to step out."

Your thoughts: "I don't like praying with you." "I'm not praying for you."

Your thoughts: "I don't have to say thank you." "They didn't even say thank you to me, so I'm not saying thank you to them."

Your thoughts: "I'm stuck. I will never get ahead."

Your thoughts: "Continue to guide me, Lord. Continue to keep me strong."

Your thoughts: "Lord, I don't feel like you love me. I hope I didn't disappoint you."

Your thoughts: "I wonder how it feels to have sex with her/him."

Your thoughts: "Lord, I have peace with this; but Lord, it hurts."

Your thoughts: "Dear God, give me the boldness and the assertiveness to do what I need to do and say what I need to say."

Your thoughts: "I'm tired of being worked on."

Your thoughts: "I realize I have an anger problem." "I get easily frustrated."

Your situation: "I know I'm right. I tend to be right in a lot of things."

Your thoughts: "Lord, help me not to take things personally; they hurt my feelings, they really said some harsh things to me."

Your thoughts: "But Lord, it hurts."

Your thoughts: "No, I don't want to read the Bible with you."

Your thoughts: "He complains too much."

Your thoughts: "I will be obedient in the midst of this pain."

Your thoughts: "Sometimes I think my meekness is being looked at as a weakness in others' eyes." "I am gentle and kind." "I don't want to despise my meekness."

Your thoughts: "I just want to feel loved and appreciated by those that I care about."

Your thoughts: "I hate her/him."

Your thoughts: "I believed when you said, 'This is not how the story ends.' "

Your thoughts: "Lord, I just want a job that pays well."

Your thoughts: "Lord, I am tired of struggling."

Your thoughts: "I just want to tell them off."

Your thoughts: "I enjoy watching spooky movies."

Yours thoughts: "Sometimes I just don't feel apart with your friends"

Your thoughts: Friends that follow worldly ways: "But they are my friends. I don't want to stop hanging around them."

Your thoughts: "I'm not ready to give up my life for the church. Let me get my life together first" "I'll think about it."

Your thoughts: "Dear Lord, I don't know about this transition in my life."

Your Thoughts: "I don't think I can be a leader."

Your thoughts: "I need to be more consistent in my walk with the Lord."

Your thoughts: "Stop being so sensitive!" (Saying to self)

Your thoughts: "Stop being so sensitive!" (If someone says this to you)

Your thoughts: "I got this job because of me; I put in the hard work to get this job, to make this kind of money."

Your thoughts: "My child can be so challenging at times."

Your thoughts: "I hate her!"

Your thoughts: "That's what he gets. He got what's coming to him."

Your thoughts: "I don't think this is going to happen. It's impossible for me to think this can happen for/to me."

Your thoughts: "I feel like all my joy is gone."

Your thoughts: "Dear God, I pray that I did not hinder my blessing or delay my promise with my foolishness. I'm so sorry, Lord."

Your thoughts: Constant negative habit of saying, "I don't have any money. I can't afford that."

Your thoughts: "I will continue to embrace your love while I wait."

Your thoughts: "I don't have to continue with this thought. Help me, Lord. Renew my mind."

Your thoughts: "Lord, I'm afraid of this. I'm worried. I'm so discouraged now."

Your thoughts: "I tend to take things personally."

Your thoughts: "So many suggestions, so many opinions. What is he going to say? I'm worrying about what people will say."

Your thoughts: "I can't. I don't know how to."

Your thoughts: "Lord, I don't know where to begin. I want my life to change."

Your thoughts: "Lord, please forgive me for not paying my tithes. I ask for mercy, Jesus."

Your thoughts: "Lord, thanks for not changing. People around me have changed and are acting funny around me."

Your thoughts: "Lord, I don't feel you are near me during this situation."

Your thoughts: "My thoughts are out of control."

Your thoughts: "He is getting on my nerves. I don't have patience for that."

Your thoughts: "I want to be so frustrated. I'm irked!"

Your thoughts: "He/she will never change."

Your thoughts: "Lord, I want to give up now. I'm tired of going through this."

Your thoughts: "I don't feel I need to bless them, they don't believe in God."

Your thoughts: "I'm materialistic."

Your thoughts: When you are having negative thoughts about someone and you are about to say those negative things.

Your thoughts: "I know that I'm going through a transition, Lord, because you told me that, 'you are going through a transition.' "

Your Thoughts: "Lord, I know you are with me and you understand my pain: pain of rejection, pain of someone I care about not liking me anymore."

Scriptures for your thoughts:

Your thoughts: "But Lord, they are not going to listen to me. They will look at me funny."

Scriptures for your thoughts: Ezekiel 2:6-7 "And thou, son of man, be not afraid of them, neither be afraid of their words though briers and thorns be with thee, and thou dost dwell among scorpions: be not afraid of their words, nor be dismayed at their looks, though they be a rebellious house. And thou shalt speak my words unto them, whether they will hear, or whether they will forbear: for they are most rebellious."

Extra encouragement: Sometimes we must be an example or share our faith with unkind people, whether they listen or not: in season and out of season or when it is inconvenient. God's strength is powerful enough to help us live for Him even under the heaviest criticism. Insecurity can get in the way of our victory. The Israelites were blessed to have the land of milk and honey, but fear, insecurity, and bondage overshadowed their promise. They could not identify their blessing. They kept the wilderness mindset.

Your thoughts: "I pray that I don't go to hell because of my dad's sins."

Scriptures for your thought s: Ezekiel 18:20 "The soul that sinneth it shall die. The son shall not bear the iniquity of the father, neither shall his father bear the iniquity of the son: the righteousness of the righteous shall be upon him and the wickedness of the wicked shall be upon him."

Just a thought: You can't be bound and liberated at the same time. Either you are free or not. You have liberty through Christ. Let go of that bondage.

Your thoughts: "God, I can't. Every time I think something is going my way, something always happens."

Scriptures for your thoughts: Luke10:19 "Behold, I give unto you power to tread on serpents and scorpions, and over all the power of the enemy: and nothing shall by any means hurt you."

Just a thought: Thank God we do not have to beg God to give us power. We as Christians are given power by God. He gave us the authority and the powerful assertiveness to cast away evil thoughts and sinful desires. You have the power within. You have the faith within. Tap into it; you already have the gifts. Utilize it. God is in control. Nothing over-shadows God's authority in this universe. Keep the faith despite what you see; despite what you know; despite what you hear; despite your situation keep the faith. Stand still and trust God!

Your thoughts: "God, I just want your Will to be manifested in my life. Let your Will be done, Lord. My will is trying to get strong."

Scriptures for your thoughts: 1 Peter 1:14-15 "As obedient children, not fashioning yourselves according to the former lusts in your ignorance; But as he which hath called you is holy, so be ye holy in all manner of conversation; Because it is written, Be ye holy; for I am holy."

Just a thought: Train your spirit through God's Words. Do what the Word says. You have to do it all the time; this must be a habit. Somebody has to be under subjection, and it's not God. Your importance of self needs to decrease. Your will must represent God's authority. You must be subservient to God—all of you, spirit, soul, and body. You have to pray and submit your will to God. You must have a heart to know God's heart. Deny yourself. Self got to die daily.

Your thoughts: "I'm tired of thinking negatively all the time. I just want peace in my mind."

Scriptures for your thoughts: 2 Corinthians 10:5 "Casting down imaginations, and every high thing that exalted itself against the knowledge of God, and bringing into captivity every thought to the obedience of Christ."

Psalms 139:23 "Search me, O God, and know my heart: try me, and know my thoughts."

Jeremiah 29:11 "For I know the thoughts that I think toward you, saith the Lord, thoughts of peace, and not evil, to give you an expected end."

Isaiah 26:3 "Thou wilt keep him in perfect peace, whose mind is stayed on thee: because he trusteth in thee."

Romans 8:6 "For to be carnally minded is death; but to be spiritually minded is life and peace."

Philippians 4:7 "And the peace of God, which passeth all understanding, shall keep your hearts and minds through Christ Jesus."

Some encouragement: What is the source of your thoughts? Where do they come from? Will your thoughts take you the way you should go according to God's will? You have the power to decide your own thoughts. Practice righteous thinking. You have the power to think Godly thoughts. You have the power to reject the ungodly thoughts. Allow

God to work in your life by believing, trusting, and having faith in Him, in His Word. If you don't like the way you think, God can change your thoughts—if you let Him. Examine your thoughts and determine if they are pleasing to God. If they are not, cast them down!

Your thoughts: "I'm not going to forgive her. I'm good."

Scriptures for your thoughts: Genesis 50:17 "... Forgive, I pray thee now, the trepass of thy brethren, and their sin; for they did unto thee evil: and now, we pray thee, forgive the trepass of the servants of the God of thy Father."

Matthew 6:14-15 "For if ye forgive men their trespasses, your heavenly Father will also forgive you: But if ye forgive not men their trespasses, neither will your Father forgive your trespasses."

Luke 6:37 "Judge not, and ye shall not be judged: condemn not, and ye shall not be condemned: forgive, and ye shall be forgiven."

28

Some encouragement: Some of us have problems admitting that we are hurting as a result of someone doing something wrong towards us. We may choose not to address it, and we will try to cover up the hurt. We'll do everything possible to cover up the hurt by drinking, smoking, not forgiving, projecting the anger elsewhere, over eating, etc. God wants us to put away all bitterness and anger. He wants us to be kind to one another and forgiving of one another.

Your thoughts: "I'm tired. I just want rest. I'm tired of being worked on by God."

Scriptures for your thoughts: Jeremiah 17:5 "This is what the Lord says: "Cursed is the one who trusts in man, who depends on flesh for his strength and whose heart turns away from the Lord.""

Galatians 6:9 "... and let us not be weary in well doing: for in due season we shall reap if we faint not."

Your thoughts: "I'm fearful."

***Scriptures for your thought*s:** 1 John 4:18 "There is no fear in love; but perfect love casteth out fear: because fear hath torment. He that fearth is not made perfect in love."

2 Timothy 1:7 "For God hath not given us the spirit of fear, but of power and of love and of a sound mind."

Your thoughts: "I want revenge! I'm going to get them back."

Scriptures for your thoughts: Proverbs 24:29 "Say not, I will do so to him as he hath done to me: I will render to the man according to his work."

Your thoughts: "She/he deserves it. Good, that's what he/she gets."

Scriptures for your thoughts: Proverbs 24:17, 18 "Rejoice not when thine enemy falleth, and let not thine heart be glad when he stumbleth: Lest the Lord see it and it displease him, and he turn away his wrath from him."

Your thoughts: "I can't believe she got the job. I'm more qualified than she is."

Scriptures for your thoughts: Proverbs 24:19, 20 "Fret not thyself because of evil men neither be thou envious at the wicked; for there shall be no reward to the evil man; the candle of the wicked shall be put out."

James 5:9 "Grudge not one against another, brethren lest ye be condemned."

James 5:11 "... the Lord is very pitiful and of tender mercy."

Your thoughts: "I'll trust you, Lord."

Scriptures for your thoughts: Psalm 18:1-3 "The Lord is my rock, and my fortress and my deliverer my God, my strength in whom I will trust. I will call upon the Lord, who is worthy to be praised, so shall I be saved from mine enemies."

Proverbs 3:5 "Trust in the Lord with all your heart and lean not on your own understanding."

Your thoughts: "I need you now, Lord."

Scriptures for your thoughts: Psalms 18:6 "In my distress I called upon the Lord, and cried unto my God, he heard my voice out of his temple, and my cry came before him even into his ears."

Psalm 28:7 "The Lord is my strength and my shield, my heart trusts Him and I am helped. My heart leaps for joy and I will give thanks to Him in song."

Psalms 31:14 "But I trust in you, O Lord; I say, "you are my God."

Psalm 32:10 ". . . but the Lord's unfailing Love surrounds the man who trusts in him."

Psalm 37:3 "Trust in the Lord and do good."

Psalm 56:3 "When I am afraid, I will trust in you."

Your thoughts: "I want to be an example of my Lord and Savior."

Scriptures for your thoughts: Matthew 5:15 "Let your light so shine before men, that they may see your good works, and glorify your Father which is in heaven."

Some encouragement: Stay focused—spiritually

Your thoughts: "My plans never come through." "No matter how much I try, something always comes up." "I knew this would happen." "I can't seem to get ahead."

Scriptures for your thoughts: 2 Corinthians 5:17 "Therefore if any man be in Christ, he is a new creature: old things are passed away; behold, all things are become new."

Philippians 2:14 "Do all things without murmurings and disputings."

Romans 12:2 "And be not conformed to this world: but be ye transformed by the renewing of your mind, that ye may prove what is that good, and acceptable, and perfect, will of God."

Philippians 4:7-9

> And the peace of God, which passeth all understanding, shall keep your hearts and minds through Christ Jesus. 8 Finally, brethren, whatsoever things are true, whatsoever things are honest, whatsoever things are just, whatsoever things are pure, whatsoever things are lovely, whatsoever things are of good report; if there be any

virtue, and if there be any praise, think on these things. 9 Those things, which ye have both learned, and received, and heard, and seen in me, do: and the God of peace shall be with you.

Some encouragement: Rejoice in the Lord right in the midst of the heavy burden trials of life. Any time we don't get what we want, some of us embrace self-pity spirits and we think negatively. We must think positively! Be ye transformed by the renewing of your mind. Be careful what you think; if you set the atmosphere of negativity, more than likely your atmosphere will be negative. You choose how your environment will be set, whether positive or negative. We must think of things that are righteous; you must walk in God's light despite the situation. Read and meditate on the Word. Negative thinking can be turned into good. Don't condemn, don't become a complainer, don't be a fault-finder. You are a new person now. It is a new day. You are a new creature in Christ. Walk in your calling. If you are a negative person, admit it! Come clean! Admit it, repent, and walk in your purpose. Satan wants you to think something is wrong with you. He wants you to think on those negative thoughts over and over and over to the point you will end up believing them. Foolishness! God has a purpose for you, so lean on Him. He will cause you to be positive. Be around positive people. God will relieve you, but you have to go to Him and let Him.

Your thoughts: "I want to hear from you, Lord."

Scriptures for your thought*s:* Psalms 46:1 "God is our refuge and strength, a very present help in trouble."

Psalms 50:3 "Our God shall come and shall not keep silence … "

Psalms 71:1 "I cried unto God with my voice, even unto God with my voice: and he gave ear unto me."

Your thoughts: "I'm sorry for my sins, Lord. I'm so sorry, Lord. Please forgive me."

Scriptures for your thought**s:** Psalms 51:1-3 "Have mercy upon me, O God, according to thy loving kindness: according unto the multitude of thy tender mercies bot out my transgressions. Wash me thoroughly from mine iniquity, and cleanse me from my sin. For I acknowledge my transgressions: and my sin is ever before me."

Psalms 51:10 "Create in me a clean heart, O God: and renew a right spirit within me."

Psalms 84:11 "For the Lord God is a sun and shield: the Lord will give grace and glory: no good thing will he withhold from them that walk uprightly."

Psalms 84:12 "O Lord of hosts, blessed is the man that trusteth in thee."

Your thoughts: "Lord, please help my friend."

Scriptures for your thoughts: Ephesians 4:2-3 "With all lowiness and meekness, with longsuffering, forbearing one another in love; Endeavoring to keep the unity of the Spirit in the bond of peace."

Encouragement: No one is ever going to be perfect here on Earth. We have to learn how to accept and love other Christians in spite of their errors and/or faults. When we see faults in our brothers and sisters in Christ; we should be patient, meek, and gentle towards them. Is there someone whose actions or personality really annoys you? Rather than harping on the person's weaknesses or faults, pray for that person. Do even more for them, spend time with them, and see if you can learn to like him or her.

Additional encouragement: We must learn to help restore our friends and loved ones to a relationship that is right with God. Allow God to restore gentleness so you won't be tempted to be angry or hold bitterness: be willing to get involved in their life with Godly boundaries. Be in the position to help them. Have the right purpose in mind to love them, to support them, to pray for them, and to restore them with God's strength. Love one another. Love covers a multitude of sin. Demonstrate Christ for them and before them. Be willing to accept them as they are; be more forgiving. God's love will have us look at others' potential in life instead of their flaws. Ye who are spiritual be spiritually-minded in your walk. Help restore them in the spirit of gentleness. Have the attitude of gentleness instead of harshness. God will let you know the right time to talk to the person. He will let you know how to respond and not to respond—what to say and what not to say. You must rely on the Holy Spirit.

Your thoughts: "I have such a desire to be accepted by others. At times, I even find myself waiting on them to validate or recognize me."

***Scriptures for your thought**s*: Matthew 5:13-14, 16 "Ye are the salt of the earth... Ye are the light of the world... Let your light so shine before men, that they may see your good works, and glorify your Father which is in heaven."

My thoughts: This is what I learned: God is the only author of the beginning and the end. God is in control; He died for us. He is in us all, which makes us loving (already), beautiful (already), strong (already), faithful (already), secured (already), fruitful (already), just (already), powerful (already), ambitious (already), loved (already), nice (already), forgiving (already), compassionate (already), humble (already), meekful (already), important (already). So why do we need someone to validate us? If we have the Lord in us already, then He is our true validation; these things are already in us. No need to have someone confirm or validate what's already in us. What you are seeking to make you feel important, secured, beautiful, etc. is already in you because God is in us and through us. We don't need others to define us to make ourselves feel good or secure. Do we or should we appreciate others' kind words, encouragement and praise? Sure, but we shouldn't rely or depend on them. We must rely on God: His Word, His Love, His validation, His approval and His directive. He died for us; He lives in us. No need to fear, no need to fret. You are beautiful because your heavenly Father is beautiful.

Your thoughts: "Lord, your peace is what I seek. Your strength is what I need right now. Your love is greatly needed to overwhelm this pain."

Scriptures for your thoughts: Psalms 5:1-3 "Give ear to my words, O Lord, consider my meditation. Hearken unto the voice of my cry, my King, and my God: for unto thee will I pray. My voice shalt thou hear in the morning. O Lord: in the morning will I direct my prayer unto thee, and will look up."

My thoughts: "Always remember, you can either become your environment or your environment becomes you" (Apostle Warren D. Martin, Sr). You control your environment with the strength and with the love of God. Cast your cares, hurt, pain, disappointments, bitterness, unforgiving hearts, and anger to the Lord. Change your environment. Be proactive. If you utilize God's peace within you, then you will have a peaceful environment. You have to believe and surround yourself with scriptures relating to peace—God's peace. When you are feeling heavy, reach, press, reach and press towards God, right in the midst of the thing. Cloudy days: press. Weary days: press. Lonesome days: press. Press right through that valley of shadow of death, that fear, that discomfort; press even when you don't want to, even when you don't feel like it. Press and step out of faith. Trust me, it will be a beautiful thing!

Your thoughts: "I trust you, Lord."

Scriptures for your thoughts: Psalms 18:1-2, 6 "I will love thee, O Lord, my strength. The Lord is my Rock, and my fortress, and my deliverer; my God, my strength, in whom I will trust; my buckler (shield), and the horn of my salvation, and my high tower… In my distress I called upon the Lord, and cried unto my God; he heard my voice out of his temple, and my cry came before him, even into his ears."

Your thoughts: "Lord, I know you are comforting me right now, right in the midst of my pain."

Scriptures for your thoughts: Psalms 23:4 "Yea, though I walk through the valley of the shadow of death, I will fear no evil: for thou art with me; thy rod and thy staff they comfort me."

Your thoughts: "I have resentment towards them."

Scriptures for your thoughts: Hebrews 12:14 "Follow peace with all men, and holiness, without which no man shall see the Lord." James 4:14-18

But if ye have bitter envying and strife in your hearts, glory not, and lie not against the truth. This wisdom desceneth not from above, but is earthly, sensual, devilish. For where envying and strife is, there is confusion and every evil work. But the wisdom that is from above is first pure, then peaceable, gentle, and easy to be intreated, full of mercy and good fruits, without partiality, and without hypocrisy.

Encouragement: It takes faith to be humble and to forgive. Pride will isolate you and break your humility. Without humility, something else is taking control: pride, fear, unforgiving. Faith works with accountability, and it will take you to another level in God. God works in accountability. There needs to be accountability in your life. Allow the Holy Spirit to inspect you. Humble yourself in the mighty hand of God. Until you become like the dying Christ, you can't be like the rising Christ. You have to die, "self." The "I" has to die to Christ daily. My Apostle Warren D. Martin Sr. once said, "Christ died once, but we die daily." Let the bitterness, anger, and discomfort die. Let it go! It's not pleasing to God, and you would not have any peace.

Your thoughts: "Dear Lord, I am so confused."

_Scriptures for your thought_s: Psalms 91:2 "I will say of the Lord, He is my refuge (shelter) and my fortress: my God: in him will I trust."

Your thoughts: "No one loves me; no one cares about me."

Scriptures for your thoughts: Psalms 100:1-5

Make a joyful noise unto the Lord, all ye lands. Serve the Lord with gladness: come before his presence with singing. Know ye that the Lord he is God: it is he that hath made us, and not we ourselves; we are his people, and the sheep of his pasture. Enter into his gates with thanksgiving, and into his courts with praise: be thankful unto him, and bless his name. For the Lord is good; his mercy is everlasting; and his truth endureth to all generations.

Encouragement: We serve one God: Jehovah. He is Sovereign. He knows all above all things. God loves us unconditionally. We have to be thankful unto Him always. It's all about God; be grateful unto Him. God loves us enough to send His only Son. We are always in His presence. He has adopted us; we are His children, and we are sealed with the Holy Spirit of promise. It should be a privilege to pray to God. He loves to supply our needs. God has gifted us; He has a plan for my life, and your life. He loves to be good to us. Jesus is interceding for us on our behalf, always. Try not to feel unloved because you are loved. Despite situations, despite what you feel. Always remember that God loves you. You have a purpose as to why you are alive today. When you feel unloved, I challenge you to go out and tell someone that you love them and bless them. Watch how God just interferes and intervenes in your life—instantly!

Your thoughts: "I'm so lonely, Lord. I know you are here with me, but I feel so lonely."

Scriptures for your thoughts: 1 Peter 5:7 "Casting all your care upon him: for he careth for you." Colossians 3:2 "Set your affection on things above, not on things on the earth."

Encouragement: To deal with loneliness, recognize that you are not weak and you are not alone. The one and only true God loves you. Strengthen your relationship with your Lord and Savior; grow to have a desire to build an intimate relationship with your Lord and Savior. You already know He loves you and will not ever, ever forsake you. Recall the promise of God; the Holy Spirit dwells in me, in you, in all of us. Develop a Godly relationship; refocus your attention onto God—not what you believe is an issue that has already been resolved.

Your thoughts: "He/She gets on my nerves."

Scriptures for your thoughts: Psalms 111:4 "He hath made his wonderful works to be remembered: the Lord is gracious and full of compassion."

Your thoughts: "I'm wondering if they are talking about me."

Scriptures for your thoughts: Psalms 118:6 "The Lord is on my side; I will not fear: what can man do unto me?"

Psalms 118:8 "It is better to trust in the Lord than to put confidence in man."

Your thoughts: "Lord, I want my will to line up with your will."

Scriptures for your thoughts: Psalms 119:10-11 "With my whole heart have I sought thee: O let me not wander from thy commandments. Thy word have I hid in my heart, that I might not sin against thee."

Psalms 119:16 "I will delight myself in thy statues: I will not forget thy word."

My thoughts: "I have to be obedient, Lord."

Your thoughts: "You make me sick."

Scriptures for your thoughts: Romans 8:8 "So then they that are in the flesh cannot please God."

Romans 8:14 "For as many as are led by the Spirit of God, they are the sons of God."

Your thoughts: "So you're saying I can't come back to church because I have a tattoo. I'm not coming to this church again."

***Scriptures for your thought**s*: 2 Corinthians 5:17 "Therefore if any man be in Christ, he is a new creature: old things are passed away; behold, all things are become new."

Romans 8:1-2 "There is therefore now no condemnation to them which are in Christ Jesus, who walk not after the flesh but after the Spirit. For the law of the Spirit of life in Christ Jesus hath made me free from the law of sin and death."

Your thoughts: "Lord, thank you for your encouraging Word."

Scriptures for your thoughts: Isaiah 43:2 "When you pass through the waters I will be with you and when you pass through the rivers they will not sweep over you. When you walk through the fire you will not be burned the flames will not set you ablaze."

47

Your thoughts: "This is why I don't like praying with you."

***Scriptures for your thoughts*:** Proverbs 18:21 "Death and life are in the power of the tongue."

Psalm 141:3-4 "Take control of what I say, O Lord, and guard my lips. Don't let me drift toward evil or take part in acts of wickedness. Don't let me share in the delicacies of those who do wrong."

Proverbs 17:28 "Even a fool, when he holdeth his peace, is counted wise: and he that shutteth his lips is esteemed a man of understanding."

Encouragement: "What's in your mouth?"

When we talk to others, to our friends, love ones, or adults in authority, how do we talk to them when they make us angry, make us laugh, make us sad or make us embarrassed with their words? Do we process the information first before we speak? Do we think before we respond? Or do we say any-thing that comes out of our mouths, regardless if it's a Godly thing to say or not. We have to be so conscious of the words we say to others. We have to learn how to control what we say and, if we have trouble in this area, we have to ask God to help us in this area. To help tame your tongue, surround yourself with scriptures. Put them in your book bag, your cell phones, your bedroom, your bedroom mirrors, somewhere you can get a quick glance or a quick reminder of God's Word about controlling your tongue. Saying the right thing according to God's Word can change your life, your situation, your atmosphere. It can change a stressful, negative moment into something peaceful and loving. Speak life into your situation and into your mind. There's power in the tongue. Proverbs 18:21 says, "Death and life are in the power of the tongue." If you speak negative words or prophecy, you will reap from what you sow and, when you are doing this, you tend to lack faith in God and you are not pleasing God. You are not allowing the Holy Spirit to edify God's word into your spirit. Psalm 141:3-4 says, "Take control of what I say, O Lord, and guard my lips. Don't let me drift toward evil or take part in acts of wickedness. Don't let me share in the delicacies of those who do wrong."

The words you say are expressions you feel in your heart. Your words can reveal imperfections within you. Ask God for help. Ask the Lord to make your heart disinclined to do evil. Who all needs help in this area, or knows someone that needs help in this area? How do you handle situations when someone is speaking evil to you or negative words about something or someone?

There are times we speak out of emotions. Yes, we are emotional beings, but we have to control our emotions to cater to God's Word. The Lord says in Philippians 4:8, "Finally, brethren, whatsoever things are true, whatsoever things are honest, whatsoever things are just, whatsoever things are pure, whatsoever things are lovely, whatsoever things are of good report; if there be any virtue, and if there be any praise, think on these things." We need to say and meditate on scripture such as these daily to keep our minds fresh with the Word so we can produce fruits with our lips. It will take practice, love, practice, love, practice, love and equally importantly forgiveness and patience. We have to plant Godly seeds. Godly wisdom. We must plant His words into our spirit and into others. God said He will add the increase; speak the Word, speak what pleases the Lord, not your flesh or to please man. We have to be honest and speak boldly before the throne. Be encouraged and be assertive to speak God's truth in all situations—no matter how small or big. It's very important for all of us to learn how to speak God's Word and not just say things based on our feelings, or even what others have said about us. We need to stop saying, "Oh, I didn't mean that. I was just kidding." We need to start being accountable for the words we speak, especially if your words hurt others. Luke 6:45 says, " A good man out of the good treasure of his heart bringeth forth that which is good; and an evil man out of the evil treasure of his heart bringeth forth the which is evil: for the abundance of the heart his mouth speaketh." So what's in your mouth: wicked seeds or Godly fruits?

Your thoughts: "These people make me sick. They are so rude and unprofessional."

***Scriptures for your thought**s:* 1 John 4:20-21 "If a man say, I love God, and hateth his brother, he is a liar: for he that loveth not his brother whom he hath seen, how can he love God whom he hath not seen? And this commandment have we from him, That he who loveth God love his brother also."

Proverbs 17:17 "A friend loveth at all times."

Your thoughts: "Lord, help me to manage my emotions better." "I'm so worried right now." "I'm scared to do it."

Scriptures for your thoughts: 1 John 4:18 "There is no fear in love; but perfect love castesth out fear: because fear hath torment. He that feareth is not made perfect in love."

Encouragement: Dear foolishness fear: I'm so sick of you trying to get me to believe that you rule and reign over my life situations, and that you have power over my finances, my life, my thoughts. You are false and you will never be life, and you will never be true. Stop trying to have me think that you have control over every situation in my life—my every move, my every thought, my every emotion. You don't! You have no power. Don't get it twisted. God did not give us the Spirit of fear, but of peace, love, and sound minds. You are dark, and I have no place for you in my light of life. You may as well take your hands off of my loved one's lives; stay out of our minds in the mighty name of Jesus! I plea the blood of Jesus over my life and my love one's lives. We have no room for you, and you are weak. We are filled with God's love and His grace, His gentle mercies and kindness. We will trust our Lord and Savior—sorry falseness! You may have had me for a moment, or my loved one's for a brief second, but we serve a God that's more powerful and mightier than you. You see, I can do all things through Christ that strengthens me! I have the victory. I'm good and blessed. You had your moment, now leave in the mighty name of Jesus and guess what? I will trust the Lord even in areas where you had me thinking that I was too weak to obey Him. Two snaps and a boom!

Your thoughts: "These people make me sick." "I'm tired of turning the other cheek."

<u>Scriptures for your thoughts</u>: Ephesians 4:2-3 "With all lowliness and meekness, with longsuffering, forbearing one another in love; Endeavoring to keep the unity of the Spirit in the bond of peace."

Ephesians 4:29-32

> Let no corrupt communication proceed out of your mouth, but that which is good to the use of edifying, that it may minister grace unto the hearers. And grieve not the Holy Spirit of God, whereby ye are sealed unto the day of redemption. Let all bitterness, and wrath, and anger, and clamour, and evil speaking, be put away from you, with all malice. And be ye kind one to another, tenderhearted, forgiving one another, even as God for Christ's sake hath forgiven you.

Just my two cents: Some people do get weary in well doing. I say be kind anyway. I like to think and believe that God is pleased and smiles on me when I'm kind to those who are mean or not kind to me. I want God to get the glory. Some people may be having a bad day or just don't know how to be kind. We are here to show kindness to others, so they can hopefully learn how to be kind through us. To me, that's called sowing seeds. Even if they don't say thank you, pray for them. They may not have been brought up to say thank you or please. We can be examples. If you know that you are weak in this area, press and ask God to show you your heart and expose the blockage that prevents you from being kind to others, especially if they have been rude or disrespectful towards you. Ask God to give you the strength to cast it down, break down that blockage. It's just that simple. Show kindness. It will make you feel good and, more importantly, it will please the Lord.

Your thoughts: "Lord, I'm just too scared to step out."

Scriptures for your thoughts: Isaiah 41:10 "Fear not, for I am with you: be not dismayed, for I am your God. I will strengthen you, yes, I will help you. I will uphold you with my righteous right hand . . . "

55

Your thoughts: "I don't like praying with you." "I'm not praying for you."

Scriptures for your thoughts: Ephesians 6:18 "Pray at all times (always) with all prayer and supplication in the Spirit, and watching thereunto with all perseverance and supplication for all saints."

1 Thessalonians 5:17 "Pray without ceasing."

Philippians 4:6-7 "Be careful for nothing; but in everything by prayer and supplication with thanksgiving let your requests be made known unto God. And the peace of God, which passeth all understanding, shall keep your hearts and minds through Christ Jesus."

My thoughts: Man should always pray, in and out of season, in good or bad situations. We should always pray to our Lord and Savior. There should never be a time when we don't/should not pray. Pray without ceasing. We should pray for one another and shouldn't have the bitterness in our hearts to refuse to pray for them. It's an awful thing to tell someone that you don't like or want to pray for them.

Your thoughts: "I don't have to say thank you." "They didn't even say thank you to me, so I'm not saying thank you to them."

Scriptures for your thoughts: 1 Thessalonians 5: 18-19 "In everything give thanks: for this is the will of God in Christ Jesus concerning you. Quench not the Spirit."

Your thoughts: "I'm stuck. I will never get ahead."

Scriptures for your thoughts: Luke 10:19 "Behold, I give unto you power to tread on serpents and scorpions, and over all the power of the enemy: and nothing shall any means hurt you."

Encouragement: Exercise faith today. Don't just think it, implement it. Use it. Action it. Believe in it. Embrace it. Do it! If you don't see how but believe it will come to pass, then you are on the right track. Please God more than your selfish ways, your own understanding, and your own ideas. Challenge yourself this day. Do something different. I'm going to put God first in this situation and I'm not going to doubt. I trust you Lord.

Your thoughts: "Continue to guide me, Lord. Continue to keep me strong."

Scriptures for your thoughts: *Isaiah 58:11 "And the Lord shall guide thee continually, and satisfy thy soul in drought, and make fat thy bones: and thou shalt be like a watered garden, and like a spring of water, whose waters fail not."*

Proverbs 3:26 "For the Lord shall be thy confidence, and shall keep thy foot from being taken."

Encouragement: This morning, Lord, you were on my mind because I was on Your mind. You watched me throughout the night and you imparted your Godly protection over me and my spirit. You love me so much. You care for me so much. You want to know my every thought. You want to know my every desire. You love this piece of handiwork you have created. You are patient with me. You are kind to me. Even in my wrong doings, you are forgiving and quick to love me. You won't hold grudges; you don't keep count of my errors. You will keep loving me despite of my shortcomings. You have prevented two car accidents from killing me that I'm aware of. You prevented a possible stray bullet from hitting me. You love me. You love me. "What manner of love is this?" (Thank you Pastor Tyrone "TWyse" Smack) Only God's love. God is love. I thank you and praise you so much.

Your thoughts: "Lord, I don't feel like you love me. I hope I didn't disappoint you."

***Scriptures for your thought**s*: Psalm 46:1 "God is our refuge and strength, a very present help in trouble."

Deuteronomy 4:31 "[For the Lord thy God is a merciful God] he will not forsake thee, neither destroy thee, nor forget the covenant of thy fathers which he sware unto them."

Proverbs 24:16 "For a just man falleth seven times, and rises up again… "

Encouragement: Love covers a multitude of sins. Multitude means a lot, a large number of, great quantity, a host, an abundance, masses, droves, heaps, etc. Notice these terms are innumerable— you can't count them! This tells me that our God, who is love, covers unlimited, great quantities of our sins. So why do we limit our love towards our brothers and sisters who fall short? Why aren't we covering our brothers and sisters in Christ with prayer and with humbleness? Why isn't there enough forgiveness, compassion, gentleness and love to cover one another? Why are we so quick to give up on people?

In Bible study one night, Prophetess Danette Strickland reminded us that we have to re-light the fire of God's love in our lives. We will speak dead bones mentally unto others before we pray for them or speak life unto their lives. That is not love. Choose this day to love in the midst of anything that may come your way, good or bad. If you can't, then ask God to renew your mind immediately— to give you strength, to have the Holy Spirit give you quick reminders of God's word to deal with the issue. Don't let it linger. Lord, help us to love despite of others' shortcomings, or even our own shortcomings. Our Word of God says the greatest commandment is love. So command love—just my two cents.

Your thoughts: "I wonder how it feels to have sex with her/him."

_Scriptures for your thought_s: 1 Corinthians 6:19-20 "Do you not know that your body is a temple of the Holy Spirit, who is in you, whom you have received from God? You are not your own: you were bought at a price. Therefore, honor God with your body."

1 Corinthians 7:1-2 "Now concerning the things whereof ye wrote unto me: It is good for a man not to touch a woman. Nevertheless, to avoid for-nication, let every man have his own wife, and let every woman have her own husband."

Just my two cents: I'll wait.

Your thoughts: "Lord, I have peace with this; but Lord, it hurts."

_Scriptures for your thought_s: John 14:27 "Peace I leave with you, my peace I give unto you: not as the world giveth, give I unto you. Let not your heart be troubled, neither let it be afraid."

Your thoughts: "Dear God, give me the boldness and the assertiveness to do what I need to do and say what I need to say."

Scriptures for your thoughts: Psalm 31:24 "Be of good courage, and he shall strengthen your heart, all ye that hope in the Lord."

Ephesians 3: 12 "In whom we have **boldness** and access with confidence by the faith of him."

2 Corinthians 7:4 "Great is my **boldness** of speech toward you, great is my glorying of you: I am filled with comfort, I am exceeding joyful in all our tribulation."

Encouragement: The power of prayer. Power resides in God, which He gives us. We have the confidence to do His Will, and we must trust in God. Erase all doubts out of your mind because faith without works is dead, and without it, it is impossible to please God. Pray for God's Will to be entered into your hearts. Be confident in this very thing knowing that God is on your side. (Thank you Pastor TWyse) Continue to love—yes, continue to love. Be His example in all that you do. God's

Word will not return to Him void. It takes determi-nation to be loose; it takes strength to persevere.

Your thoughts: "I'm tired of being worked on."

Scriptures for your thoughts: Romans 5:3 "And not only so, but we glory in tribulations also: knowing that tribulation worketh patience."

Romans 8:25 "But if we hope for that we see not, then do we with patience wait for it."

Galatians 5:22 "But the fruit of the Spirit is love, joy, peace, longsuffering, gentleness, goodness, faith."

Encouragement: There has to be a rebuke, a reproof in order to receive the blessing from God. He wants you to keep focus on Him while He works on you. Situations like these make you see God despite the negative circumstances. God matters first when things come up. Satan is in the midst of stealing your determination, so continue to worship, praise, and sacrifice your will unto His. God wants to correct; Satan doesn't. He wants you to abide to your flesh and selfish ways. You may have to be uncomfortable to get what God has for you. Stay focused. He is allowing situations to happen to strengthen you and to show you to yourself. No need to embrace fear anymore; embrace God's loving kindness instead.

Your thoughts: "I realize I have an anger problem." "I get easily frustrated."

Scriptures for your thoughts: Psalm 37:8 "Cease from anger, and forsake wrath: fret not thyself in any wise to do evil."

Proverbs 12:16 "A fool's wrath is presently known: but a prudent man covereth shame."

Proverbs 14:29 "He that is slow to wrath is of great understanding: but he that is hasty of spirit exalteth folly."

Proverbs 29:11 "A fool uttereth all his mind: but a wise man keepeth it in till afterwards."

Encouragement: Love your enemies; love those who want to hate you, despise you, has a distaste towards you; who hurt you; love them anyway; We must learned to love our enemies or people who are quick to anger or get easily upset. We should be concerned about other's spiritual welfare. Ephesians 4:29-32 says "Let no corrupt communication proceed out of your mouth, but that which is good to the use of edifying, that it may minister grace unto the hearers. And grieve not the holy Spirit of God, whereby ye are sealed unto the day of redemption. Let all bitterness, and wrath, and anger, and clamour, and evil speaking, be put away from you, with all malice: And be ye kind one to another, tenderhearted, forgiving one another, even as God for Christ's sake hath forgiven you." Don't think you can do it? Then ask the Lord to give you the strength to do it! You control your anger; don't let it control you.

Your thoughts: "I know I'm right. I tend to be right in a lot of things."

Scriptures for your thoughts: Philippians 2:3-4 "Let nothing be done through strife or vainglory; but in lowliness of mind let each esteem other better than themselves. Look not every man on his own things, but every man also on the things of others."

James 3:17-18 "But the wisdom that is from above is first pure, then peaceable, gentle, and easy to be intreated, full of mercy and good fruits, without partiality, and without hypocrisy. And the fruit of righteousness is sown in peace of them that make peace."

Romans 12:18 "If it be possible, as much as lieth in you, live peaceably with all men."

Encouragement: The Bible teaches us to be peacemakers. We have to practice humility to properly deal with difficult people. We have to be patient with others' shortcomings, because I'm quite sure they have to be patient with our shortcomings. This can be tough and, at times, it may feel like "it's just not right for them to treat me or others that way." I learned that people who get angry a lot usually justify their anger or bitterness by saying it's someone else's fault: "they are the blame" for my anger. "If they wouldn't have done what they did or said what they said, I wouldn't have gotten so angry." Misplacing their anger and not taking their responsibility of controlling their own emotions is what I like to call it. However, the

Bible warns us against giving in to anger/bitterness when we are upset by other people's reactions or their words towards us. When we give in to anger or allow our anger to direct our thoughts or actions, we often lose focus off of God and focus on our own selfishness or comfort. We should be compassionate, loving, and concerned about other's feelings and be good witnesses for the Lord. We should respond with gentle spirit and kindness – slow to anger. Holding on to anger is not healthy and, most importantly, it does not please our Lord and Savior.

Your thoughts: "Lord, help me not to take things personally; they hurt my feelings, they really said some harsh things to me."

Scriptures for your thoughts: 1 Corinthians 13:4-5 "Charity suffereth long, and is kind; charity envieth not; charity vaunteth not itself, is not puffed up, Doth not behave itself unseemly, seeketh not her own, is not easily provoked, thinketh no evil."

2 Corinthians 12:10 "Therefore I take pleasure in infirmities, in reproaches, in necessities, in

persecutions, in distresses for Christ's sake: for when I am weak, then am I strong."

Encouragement: I learned that we, as emotional beings, can take things personally when someone insults us, disappoint us, ignores us, or is rude to us, especially if they do it on purpose. More than likely, they may be hurt themselves; despite of the hurt and pain, ask God to give you strength to forgive, to be patient with them, and try your best to avoid taking things personally or giving in to self-pity. When you find yourself thinking insecurely or thinking thoughts of self-pity, immediately cast them down, and make them be subservient under God's authority. Wow! I learned that people who purposely try to hurt your feelings want you to take them personally. Some hurt people want to hurt others because they are hurting. We may want to find out why they may be hurting; was it something that you may have said? Are they under pressure? Are they tired or exhausted? Are they trying to get their lives together and are getting frustrated? Maybe their reaction is due to his/ her concentration on health issues, their family, etc. Maybe you may not see things clearly, or may have misinterpreted something. Here's an interesting point: did you set yourself up to be hurt? This requires some self-assessment. I'm not condoning disrespect or abuse, and if you feel that you are, please seek counseling support and services or have a talk with your minister or pastor of your church. We all want to be respected and to be loved according to God's Word.

Your thoughts: "But Lord, it hurts."

Scriptures for your thoughts: Proverbs 3:5 "Trust in the Lord with all your heart, and do not lean on your own understanding."

Numbers 23:19 "God is not man, that he should lie, or a son of man, that he should change his mind. Has he said, and will he not do it? Or has he spoken, and will he not fulfill it?"

Encouragement: You must control your environment (anger, bitterness, depression, pride, impatience, self-pity, insecurity). Don't let your environment control you. Does your voice sound like your environment? Change your attitude towards the situation. Give your pain and your hurt to the Lord. Ask the Lord to give you peace, comfort, and relief right in the midst of the situation; right in the midst of the pain, right in the midst of the matter. Give it to the Lord.

It's hard, right? That's okay. When it's hard, ask the Holy Spirit to give you the strength to let go of the matter. As a matter of fact, what is your attitude towards the problem? Are you focusing on the issue too much? What's bigger: your faith or the issue? As my Apostle Warren D. Martin, Sr. said during his sermon on June 14, 2015, "failure is not an option." You/we are victorious! Be determined to be loose from your problem. You do not have to follow the negative environment. You are more than a conquer. Who do you know? Who do you belong to? What does the Word say? Rejoice in the matter! You know God is Faithful! You've seen it too many times! God knew we would struggle with difficulties. In His Word, He lovingly points us to hope! Luke 10:19 (KJV) says, "Behold, I give unto you power to tread on serpents and scorpions, and over all the power of the enemy: and nothing shall by any means hurt you." Acts 18:10 (KJV) tells us, "For I am with thee, and no man shall set on thee to hurt thee: for I have much people in this city." God wants us to trust Him in every trial and through every trouble. Hebrews 11:6 (NIV) says, "And without faith it is impossible to please God, because anyone who comes to him must believe that he exists and that he rewards those who earnestly seek him." God cares about your struggles. Jesus said in Matthew 11:28-30 "Come unto me, all ye that labour and are heavy laden, and I will give you rest. Take my yoke upon you and learn of me; for I am meek and lowly in heart, and ye shall find rest unto your souls. For my yoke is easy, and my burden is light. "

Do you realize that some of us hurt loudly (cursing, having an attitude, complaining, selfish, self-pity) and some us hurt quietly (worrying, being depressed, being isolated, suicidal). Many of us are hurting by refusing to express our true feelings in order to save face with others. We would rather hold our true thoughts and ideas than expressing them. We are hurting ourselves by not freeing

71

our minds. We are not freeing who we truly are in God's eyes. Another example are those who complain a lot—complaining by pointing the fingers at others, and having a self-righteous attitude. Not wanting anyone to get involved can be a hurtful sign—being embarrassed, having fear of being talked about or being laughed at. We tend to keep it all in. All fearful boundaries are from the Devil. The Lord says in Hebrews 10:25, "not forsaking the assembling of ourselves together, as the manner of some is; but exhorting one another: and so much the more, as ye see the day approaching." We must find a truthful and God-fearing friend to convey our hurt to. Having a conversation with the Lord is key, but He also said in His Word that we should carry each other's burdens. Hurt/pain is that uncomfortable, unfair type of burden or feeling that we all face at times. Dealing with hurt or pain is such an uncomfortable feeling, a feeling we all wish to avoid, but we have to ask the Lord to heal our painful hearts and to learn and grow from it.

Your thoughts: "No, I don't want to read the Bible with you."

Scriptures for your thoughts: 2 Timothy 3:16-17 "All Scripture is breathed out by God and profitable for teaching, for reproof, for correction, and for training in righteousness, that the man of God may be competent, equipped for every good work."

Matthew 4:4 "But he answered and said, "It is written, Man shall not live by bread alone, but by every word that comes from the mouth of God."

1 Timothy 4:13 **"**Until I come, devote yourself to the public reading of Scripture, to exhortation, to teaching."

Just a thought: We should be prepared to read the Bible with others. For the Bible says 2 Timothy 4:2 "Preach the word; be instant in season, out of season; reprove, rebuke, exhort with all long suffering and doctrine." Why wouldn't you want to read the Word with others? Why wouldn't you want to share how God loves us? You don't want to read the Word to others because of pride? Anger? Hurt? It's important to read the Word daily because it strengthens us, empowers us, cleanses us, directs us and draws us closer to God. It teaches us about God and His love for us. The Bible has been written for all to read, to meditate on, and to put it into action. It is our answer to all things, and it is 100% reliable. We are to spread the Word, spread the Gospel to all God's people. We should have a desire to not only read the Word, but to share the Word and to read it with others. God's Word says in Proverbs 27:17 "Iron sharpens iron, So one man sharpens another." We should not be forsaking ourselves or others.

Your thoughts: "He complains too much."

Scriptures for your thoughts: Philippians 2:14 "Do all things without murmurings and disputings."

Ephesians 4:29 **"Let no corrupt communication proceed out of your mouth, but that which is good to the use of edifying, that it may minister grace unto the hearers."**

Numbers 11:1-4 "And [when] the people complained, it displeased the LORD: and the LORD heard [it]; and his anger was kindled; and the fire of the LORD burnt among them, and consumed [them that were] in the uttermost parts of the camp."

Just my two cents: When we complain, we are being selfish and very unappreciative to God's blessing. I believe God is not pleased when we fret over His blessings (jobs, home, friends, our bodies, our personal appearances, etc.) Are you speaking life or death into your situation? If you know of someone who complains a lot, let them know that they are displeasing God, and that their situation will not change because of their negative mindset; they are being selfish. Speak life into your situation. Speak life into those dead bones. Stop using your mouth to invite the Devil into your situation. Be positive. Be encouraging. Don't be ungrateful.

Your thoughts: "I will be obedient in the midst of this pain."

Scriptures for your thoughts*: Psalm 119:11 "Thy word have I hid in my heart, that I might not sin against thee."

Just a friendly reminder: God once shared with me, "I've got this. I've got to deal with this—not you."

75

Just a thought: At times we let ourselves get all worked up and stressed out when we try to change something that is beyond our control. No one can add a single day or hour to his/her life. Thank God He loves us and holds everything in His hands, including our stressful, painful and out-of-control situations.

Your thoughts: "Sometimes I think my meekness is being looked at as a weakness in others' eyes." "I am gentle and kind." "I don't want to despise my meekness."

Scriptures for your thought*s:* Isaiah 53:7 "He was oppressed, and he was afflicted, yet he opened not his mouth: he is brought as a lamb to the slaughter, and as a sheep before her shearers is dumb, so he openeth not his mouth."

Matthew 5:5 "Blessed are the meek: for they shall inherit the earth."

Encouragement: It's a positive trait and character of God—don't despise your meekness. Allow Him to mold you; He is trying to teach you. Yes, it is painful at times, but it is positive; it is a process.

He wants you to know how to recognize it. It is a great value and meekness is a fruit of the spirit; you have to be processed. (Thank you so much Sister Rachel)

Your thoughts: "I just want to feel loved and appreciated by those that I care about."

***Scriptures for your thought**s*: Ephesians 3:16 "That he would grant you, according to the riches of his glory, to be strengthened with might by his Spirit in the inner man; That Christ may dwell in your hearts by faith; that ye, being rooted and grounded in love."

Just my two cents: Know that God loves you always, flaws and all. He created you, so He already knows your weaknesses, strengths, likes, dislikes, what makes you angry and what makes you smile. Focus on His love. Cast down those imaginary thoughts that are wearing you down, that makes you feel depressed or stressed. God cares about you so much. Read His Word and you will learn how much He loves and adores us all. Our friends and family can't be depended upon to fill the void that you want filled. Their love can be conditional, brief, limited and unpredictable. To feel validated, to feel included, to feel appreciated, and to feel loved should only be fulfilled by God. He is consistent, unchangeable, and reliable, and can make you feel whole with His love.

Your thoughts: "I hate her/him."

Scriptures for your thoughts: Ephesians 4:29-32

Let no corrupt communication proceed out of your mouth, but that which is good to the use of edifying, that it may minister grace unto the hearers. And grieve not the Holy Spirit of God, whereby ye are sealed unto the day of redemption. Let all bitterness, and wrath, and anger, and clamour, and evil speaking, be put away from you, with all malice: And be ye kind one to another, tenderhearted, forgiving one another, even as God for Christ's sake hath forgiven you.

Just some thoughts: Don't give up on love because someone may need it. Don't give up on prayer or sharing God's Word because someone may need it. Love all, but with God's love not the worldly love.

Your thoughts: "I believed when you said Lord, 'This is not how the story ends.' "

Scripture for your thought: Psalms 62:8 "Trust in him at all times; ye people, pour out your heart before him: God is a refuge for us, Selah."

My two cents: God's Word supersedes the world's way all the time! Always remember that God is our refuge. Read and study this scripture when you don't feel like it; when you are going through hard times, while you are pressing, or when you need encouragement. Don't believe that God's Word is never needed when you are going through something. His Word is needed all the time, in and out of season.

Your thoughts: "Lord, I just want a job that pays well."

Scriptures for your thoughts: Mark 11:23-24 "Truly I say to you, whoever says to this mountain,

'Be taken up and cast into the sea,' and does not doubt in his heart, but believes that what he says is going to happen, it will be granted him. Therefore I say to you, all things for which you pray and ask, believe that you have received them, and they will be granted you."

Your thoughts: "Lord, I am tired of struggling."

Scriptures for your thoughts: Matthew 11:29-30 "Take my yoke upon you, and learn of me; for I am meek and lowly in heart; and ye shall find rest unto your souls. For my yoke is easy and my burden is light."

Psalm 37:3-4 "Trust in the LORD and do good; Dwell in the land and cultivate faithfulness. Delight yourself in the LORD; And He will give you the desires of your heart."

My two cents: Lord, despite of what I see, despite of what I feel, despite of what I know, despite of what I hear, I will still trust you. I will have faith in you.

Your thoughts: "I just want to tell them off."

Scriptures for your thoughts: Galatians 5:22-23 "But the fruit of the spirit is love, joy, peace, long-suffering, gentleness, goodness, faith, meekness, temperance: against such there is no law."

Ephesians 4:2 "With all lowliness and meekness, with longsuffering, forbearing one another in love."

Your thoughts: "I enjoy watching spooky movies."

Scriptures for your thoughts: 1 Timothy 6:11-12 "But thou, O man of God, flee these things; and follow after righteousness, Godliness, faith, love, patience, meekness."

Yours thoughts: "Sometimes I just don't feel apart with your friends"

Scriptures for your thoughts: Isaiah 41:10 "Fear thou not; for I am with thee: be not dismayed: for I am thy God; I will strengthen thee: yea, I will help thee; yea, I will uphold thee with the right hand of my righteousness."

Your thoughts: Friends that follow worldly ways: "But they are my friends. I don't want to stop hanging around them."

Scriptures for your thoughts: Ephesians 5:1, 8 & 11 "Be ye therefore followers of God, as dear children." "For ye were sometimes darkness, but now are ye light in the Lord: walk as children of light:" "And have no fellowship with the unfruitful works of darkness, but rather reprove them."

My two cents: Don't follow people who walk in ungodly spirits. They will darken your spirit and alienate you from God with their wicked ways. Don't walk with them or act like them but instead, be a light before them and an example of Christ. Be a leader and follower of Christ.

Your thoughts: "I'm not ready to give up my life for the church. Let me get my life together first" "I'll think about it."

Scriptures for your thoughts: Romans 12:2 " And be not conformed to this world: but be ye transformed by the renewing of your mind, that ye may prove what is that good, and acceptable, and perfect will of God."

My thoughts: Submit or give up your wicked ways and don't conform to this world. It is temporal. Turn your life to God; put your care, your strength, your struggles, your faith, and burdens into the Lord's hand. Renew your mind today! Tomorrow is not promised to anyone. Allow the Lord to shape and mold you; to create a new mind and heart in you. Don't get content with the world. It will not save you from the wrath of hell!

Your thoughts: "Dear Lord, I don't know about this transition in my life."

Scriptures for your thoughts: Isaiah 41:10 "Fear thou not; for I am with thee: be not dismayed: for I am thy God, I will strengthen thee: yea, I will help thee; yea, I will uphold thee with the right hand of my righteousness."

Encouragement: Dear Lord, I don't know if I'm ready for this transition, but I believe you know I'm ready. Continue to guide me and direct my path. You know the plans you have for my life, so I trust you. I have faith in you. I rely on you to pull me through this. This transition will be for my good. I may not know all the details, and I don't have all the facts or evidence, but that's just the beauty of faith. I know I'll be at peace. I know it will feel like a dream. Thank you, Lord, for using this vessel, the undeserved servant of God. I love you, and I'm ready. Love, your special one. You still choose me, and I'm totally grateful.

Your Thoughts: "I don't think I can be a leader."

***Scriptures for your thought**s:* Deuteronomy 5: 31 "But as for thee, stand thou here by me, and I will speak unto thee all the commandments, and the statues, and the judgements, which thou shalt teach them that they may do them in the land which I give them to possess it."

Joshua 1:9 "Have not I commanded thee? Be strong and of a good courage; be not afraid, neither be thou dismayed: for the Lord thy God is with thee whithersoever thou goest."

Food for thought (me): You may have the wrong people in your court, in your corner, on your ship.

As a leader, who believes in your vision? Who supports your vision? Who wants to help implement your vision? Well, as a leader, you have to see who is in your court, who is in your corner. You may have the wrong people surrounding you. Take inventory. Who needs coaching? Who needs discipline to better understand your vision, your goals, your plans? Feed your team; feed them the Word. Neglect not the fellowship of the saints. Keep focus. Don't let what God has in you fall to the ground because of your heart. You cannot afford to be lost or unfocused. As a leader, God's vessel, child of God, you cannot be afraid to fail or to drive the vision that God gave you. Because of you, your followers and your supporters will learn what not to do and what they can do per God's Word. You can't walk with fear; just implement your plan that God has for you without fear. As a leader, make sure you have a church that will cover you and that will hold you accountable. You must have a place to worship. God wants to appoint a place for His people. All leaders need to be covered and to be humble enough to follow. As a leader, you are here for a reason. You have been chosen for a reason. Embrace your gift. Embrace your calling.

Your thoughts: "I need to be more consistent in my walk with the Lord."

***Scriptures for your thought**s*: Psalm 51:10-12 "Create in me a clean heart, O God: and renew a right spirit within me. Cast me not away from thy presence, and take not thy holy spirit from me. Restore unto me the joy of thy salvation; and uphold me with thy free spirit."

My two cents: If you want to be delivered, you must be consistent—consistent with prayer, reading your Word, fellowshipping with others, consistent in doing the right things. Apostle Warren D. Martin, Sr. said, "We need some good old fashion resistance." Resist the devil and he will flee. Are you connected to a vision? Are you winning souls to Christ? Your leader(s) must challenge you to walk spiritually. You will appear very insecure when you don't show secureness. Walk in your full potential.

Your thoughts: "Stop being so sensitive!" (Saying to self)

Scriptures for your thoughts: Psalm 62:6-8 "He only is my rock and my salvation: he is my defense, I shall not be moved. In God is my salvation and my glory: the rock of my strength, and my refuge, is in God. Trust in Him at all times; ye people, pour out your heart before him: God is a refuge for us. Selah."

Your thoughts: "Stop being so sensitive!" (If someone says this to you)

Scriptures for your thoughts: Matthew 11: 29 "Take my yoke upon you and learn of me: for I am meek and lowly in heart and ye shall find rest unto your souls."

Your thoughts: "I got this job because of me; I put in the hard work to get this job, to make this kind of money."

Scriptures for your thoughts: Proverbs 11:28 "He that trusteth in his riches shall fall: but the righteous shall flourish as a branch."

Proverbs 13:7 "There is that maketh himself rich, yet hath nothing: there is that maketh himself poor, yet hath great riches."

Proverbs 23:4 "Labour not to be rich: cease from thine own wisdom."

Your thoughts: "My child can be so challenging at times."

***Scriptures for your thought*s:** Proverbs 22:6 "Train up a child in the way he should go; and when he is old, he will not depart from it."

Just my two cents: Please, do not call your child or anyone's child out of their names "bad child," or say she is so mean," etc. What you feed your child they may become just that. If you call your child a bad seed, they just may believe that and act on that name. Instead, feed them God's Word, he/she will be a child of God. Ask God for strength for those difficult times when raising your children.

Your thoughts: "I hate her!"

Scriptures for your thoughts: Proverbs 10:12 "Hatred stirreth up strifes: but love covereth all sins."

Your thoughts: "That's what he gets. He got what's coming to him."

Scriptures for your thoughts: Proverbs 24:17-18 "Rejoice not when thine enemy falleth, and let not thine heart be glad when he stumbleth: Lest the Lord see it, and it displease him and he turn away his wrath from him."

My two cents: Be nice!

Your thoughts: "I don't think this is going to happen. It's impossible for me to think this can happen for/to me."

Scriptures for your thought*s:* Luke 18:27 "And he said, the things which are impossible with men are possible with God."

Your thoughts: "I feel like all my joy is gone."

Scriptures for your thoughts: Nehemiah 8:10 " . . . for this day is holy unto our Lord: neither be ye sorry; for the joy of the Lord is your strength."

My two cents: We didn't lose our joy; we gave it up. Always remember that God is our refuge, there is such pleasure and peacefulness in that. Joy is already in you, just tap into it and use it.

Your thoughts: "Dear God, I pray that I did not hinder my blessing or delay my promise with my foolishness. I'm so sorry, Lord."

Scriptures for your thoughts: Romans 8:28 "And we know that all things work together for good to them that love God, to them who are called according to his purpose."

My thoughts: Lord, give me the strength to starve my distractions, both big and small, and keep me focused on my purpose, the purpose you have for me. Teach me how to avoid distractions. Teach me how to recognize them to avoid them. I have to embrace and understand the process of my purpose. "We should honor our purpose" (Apostle Warren D. Martin, Sr.).

Your thoughts: Constant negative habit of saying, "I don't have any money. I can't afford that."

Scriptures for your thoughts: Mark 11:22 " . . . have faith in God."

Mark 11:24 "Therefore I say unto you, what things soever ye desire when ye pray, believe that ye receive them, and ye shall have them."

My thoughts: We are no longer in the wilderness of negative thoughts—no more wilderness mindset as the Israelites had. They still murmured and complained when they were delivered from Pharaoh's hand; they continued to complain despite being delivered, and they knew they were on their way to the Promised Land. Don't bring your negative thoughts and habits into your deliverance. You have been set free. Trust in God, not money, to get you through, to bless you of your desires. Money does not save you, God does. God will make a way for you; He will use whatever and whoever to handle your situation. Rely on God, not money. "Trust in the Lord." Say to yourself, "I no longer live in the wilderness in my mind."

Your thoughts: "I will continue to embrace your love while I wait."

Scriptures for your thoughts: Mark 12:30 "And thou shalt love the Lord thy God with all thy heart, and with all thy soul, and with all thy mind, and with all thy strength: this is the first commandment."

My thoughts: I will focus on you while I wait. I will focus on the purpose you have for me while I wait. I will focus on your love.

Your thoughts: "I don't have to continue with this thought. Help me, Lord. Renew my mind."

Scriptures for your thoughts: Romans 12:2 "And be not conformed to this world: but be ye transformed by the renewing of your mind, that ye may prove what is that good, and acceptable, and perfect, will of God."

2 Corinthians 10:5 "Casting down imaginations, and every high thing that exalteth itself against the knowledge of God, and bringing into captivity every thought to the obedience of Christ."

My two cents: You have the power to control your thoughts. God gave us the power, the strength and the gift of the Holy Spirit to help combat our negative/ungodly thoughts. You have it in you! Use the power. Combat those thoughts with God's Word.

Replace thoughts with positive thoughts, not fearful ones. "I no longer live in the wilderness in my mind."

Your thoughts: "Lord, I'm afraid of this. I'm worried. I'm so discouraged now."

Scriptures for your thoughts: Isaiah 41:10 "Fear thou not: for I am with thee: be not dismayed: for I am thy God: I will strengthen thee: yea, I will help thee: yea, I will uphold thee with the right hand of my righteousness."

Your thoughts: "I tend to take things personally."

Scriptures for your thoughts: Isaiah 54:17 " 'No weapon formed against thee shall prosper: and every tongue that shall rise against thee in judgment thou shalt condemn. This is the heritage of the servants of the Lord, and their righteousness is of me,' saith the Lord."

Your thoughts: "So many suggestions, so many opinions. What is he going to say? I'm worrying about what people will say."

Scriptures for your thoughts: Jeremiah 7:23 "But this thing commanded I them, saying, 'Obey my voice, and I will be your God, and ye shall be my people: and walk ye in all the ways that I have commanded you, that it may be well unto you.' "

Your thoughts: "I can't. I don't know how to."

Scriptures for your thoughts: Nahum 1:7 "The Lord is good, a strong hold in the day of trouble; and he knoweth them that trust in him."

Your thoughts: "Lord, I don't know where to begin. I want my life to change."

Scriptures for your thoughts: Habakkuk 2:2-3 "And the Lord answered me, and said, write the vision and make it plain upon tables, that he may run that readeth it. For the vision is yet for an appointed time, but at the end it shall speak, and not lie: though it tarry, wait for it; because it will surely come, it will not tarry."

Your thoughts: "Lord, please forgive me for not paying my tithes. I ask for mercy, Jesus."

Scriptures for your thoughts: Malachi 3:10 "Bring ye all the titles into the storehouse, that there may be meat in mine house, and prove me now herewith, saith the Lord of hosts, if I will not open you the windows of heaven, and pour you out a blessing, that there shall not be room enough to receive it."

Your thoughts: "Lord, thanks for not changing. People around me have changed and are acting funny around me."

Scriptures for your thoughts: Malachi 3:6 "For I am the Lord, I change not . . ."

My two cents: Give God a chance. He does not change! And maybe it's you that is changing and not other people.

Your thoughts: "Lord, I don't feel you near me during this situation."

Scriptures for your thoughts: Romans 8:38-39 "For I am persuaded, that neither death, nor life, nor angels, nor principalities, nor powers, nor things present, nor things to come, Nor height, nor depth, nor any other creature, shall be able to separate us from the love of God, which is in Christ Jesus our Lord."

Your thoughts: "My thoughts are out of control."

Scriptures for your thoughts: Isaiah 26:3 "Thou wilt keep him in perfect peace, whose mind is stayed on thee: because he trusteth in thee."

My two cents: You have control over your thoughts. Your thoughts do not, or should not, control you. Remember you have the power, God's power, to make a change.

Your thoughts: "He is getting on my nerves. I don't got patience for that."

Scriptures for your thoughts: 2 Corinthians 10:3-4 "For though we walk in the flesh, we do not war after he flesh: (For the weapons of our warfare are not carnal, but mighty through God to the pulling down of strong holds;)"

Your thoughts: "I want to be so frustrated. I'm irked!"

Scriptures for your thoughts: Galatians 5:22-23 "But the fruit of the Spirit is love, joy, peace, long-suffering, gentleness, goodness, faith, Meekness, temperance: against such there is no law."

Your thoughts: "He/she will never change."

Scriptures for your thoughts: Galatians 6:1-2 "Brethren, if a man be overtaken in a fault, ye which are spiritual, restore such a one in the spirit of meekness; considering thyself, lest thou also be tempted. Bear ye one another's burdens, and so fulfill the law of Christ."

Your thoughts: "Lord, I want to give up now. I'm tired of going through this."

Scriptures for your thoughts: Galatians 6:9 "And let us not be weary in well doing: for in due season we shall reap, if we faint not."

Your thoughts: "I don't feel I need to bless them, they don't believe in God."

Scriptures for your thoughts: Galatians 6:10 "As we have therefore opportunity, let us do good unto all men, especially unto them who are of the household of faith."

Your thoughts: "I'm materialistic."

Scriptures for your thoughts: Ephesians 2:8-9 "For by grace are ye saved through faith; and that not of yourselves: it is the gift of God: Not of works, lest any man should boast."

Your thoughts: When you are having negative thoughts about someone and you want to say something negative about them.

Scriptures for your thoughts: Ephesians 4:29 "Let no corrupt communication proceed out of your mouth, but that which is good to the use of edifying, that it may minister grace unto the hearers."

Your thoughts: "I know that I'm going through a transition, Lord, because you told me that, 'you are going through a transition.' "

Scriptures for your thoughts: Psalm 92:10 "I shall be anointed with fresh oil."

Encouragement: *Transition*

*I believe that many of us go through various tran-
sitions in our lives with the Lord. I truly believe that
once we embrace the Lord in any part of our lives,
we are beginning a new transition in that partic-
ular area. Just before my fiftieth birthday, the Lord
told me that I was going through a transition with
Him, newness with Him. I didn't know exactly what
that meant, but I began to be even more obser-
vant with my surroundings, my Bible study life, and
my relationship with the Lord to try to figure out
what this transition was all about. To be honest,
I'm still learning and embracing this new transition.
How many of you believe that God is touching you,
informing you that a new transition is upon you?
Just to make sure we are on the same page, I want
to share with you what I learned about what the
word "transition" means: I learned that transition is
a process or a period of changing from one state
to another. Its synonyms are change, move, trans-
formation, metamorphosis, shift, switch, leap, or
alteration. If you believe that you are beginning a
new transition with the Lord, my prayer is for you,*

and for me, is to embrace, to be obedient, and to listen to His voice during this new season.

Just to piggyback on what Apostle Warren D. Martin Sr. preached about on December 27, 2015 from the scripture Psalm 92:10, "I shall be anointed with fresh oil," many of us learned that David was excited of the new mercies, the fresh oil, a new transition with the Lord. When going through transition with the Lord with our lives, when embracing the new oil, we must be obedient and we must follow order. This transition is all about going through another level with the Lord, a level we all have not seen before. A change—a new beginning is happening.

An example of one who embarked on a transition in life was Simon. Simon's transition happened when Jesus said to him, "Follow me, and I will make you a fishers of men" (Matthew 4:19). Simon "straightway left his nets and followed Him"(Matthew 4:20). Simon's transition began once he gave up his life, his lifestyle, his ship, his father, his personal desires, his job, etc. and followed Jesus. As part of Simon's transition, the Lord changed his name from Simon to Peter. He embraced this new transition and followed Jesus. When going through a transition, we must give up our selfish desires, give up old ways in handling things, old mindsets and follow Jesus. We must listen to God's voice. (Thanks Pastor Donald Strickland)

In closing, to embrace a transition with the Lord in our lives, we must embrace His order and begin to embrace new responsibilities, new account-abilities, new goals, new plans, new implemen-tations, new environments. We must accept new levels with God, new levels of wisdom, new levels of love, new orders, new mindsets, and embrace new assertiveness, new spiritual aggressiveness, new understanding of God's word, new ways in handling criticism, new ways in addressing short-comings, new awards, new securities, new friends, and new purpose. If you believe that God is tran-sitioning you, embrace the transition, embrace the newness, embrace the fresh oil, and embrace your new level with the Lord, but be willing and ready to leave or give up your old lifestyle.

Your Thoughts: "Lord, I know you are with me and you understand my pain: pain of rejection, pain of someone I care about not liking me anymore."

Scriptures for your thoughts: Psalm 25:17-18 "The troubles of my heart are enlarged: O bring thou me out of my distresses. Look upon mine affliction and my pain; and forgive all my sins."

Psalm 18: 1-3 " . . . will love thee, O Lord, my strength. The Lord is my rock, and my fortress, and my deliverer; my God, my strength, in whom I will trust: my buckler, and the horn of my salvation, and my high tower. I will call upon the Lord, who is worthy to be praised: so shall I be saved from mine enemies."

Dear Lord, I don't know if I'm ready for this transition, but I believe you know I'm ready. Continue to guide me and direct my path. You know the plans you have for my life, so I trust you. I have faith in you. I rely on you to pull me through this. This transition will be for my good. I may not know all the details, and I don't have all the facts or evidence, but that's just the beauty of faith. I know I'll be at peace. I know it will feel like a dream. Thank you, Lord, for using this vessel, the undeserved servant of God. I love you and I'm ready. Love, your special one. "You still choose me" and I'm totally grateful. I love you.

CPSIA information can be obtained at www.ICGtesting.com
Printed in the USA
BVOW04s2315090816

458482BV00001B/1/P